MW00368495

SATs Skills

Reading Comprehension Workbook

8–9 years

OXFORD

UNIVERSITY PRESS

Different types of question

You will find several different types of questions in this book:

- short answers which need one word or a few words

- several line answers which need one or two sentences

- longer answers where you need to explain in more detail, give several points and use evidence from the text.

Some questions have multiple choice answers which may need ticking or circling. For some questions you may need to draw lines or complete a table.

Tips: Always look at the number of marks available and the amount of space provided for your answer. Use this as a guide to know how much to write.

If the question asks for evidence, make sure you include some short, relevant quotations from the text which help support your point.

Always use the text for evidence; do not rely on the pictures.

OXFORD
UNIVERSITY PRESS

Great Clarendon Street, Oxford, OX2 6DP, United Kingdom

Oxford University Press is a department of the University of Oxford. It furthers the University's objective of excellence in research, scholarship, and education by publishing worldwide. Oxford is a registered trade mark of Oxford University Press in the UK and in certain other countries

Text © Oxford University Press 2017

Author: Michellejoy Hughes

The moral rights of the author have been asserted

First published in 2017

British Library Cataloguing in Publication Data
Data available

978-0-19-274958-1

10 9 8 7 6 5 4 3 2 1

Paper used in the production of this book is a natural, recyclable product made from wood grown in sustainable forests. The manufacturing process conforms to the environmental regulations of the country of origin.

Printed in China

Acknowledgements

Cover illustration: Lo Cole
Page make-up and illustrations by Aptara

Although we have made every effort to trace and contact all copyright holders before publication this has not been possible in all cases. If notified, the publisher will rectify any errors or omissions at the earliest opportunity.

Links to third party websites are provided by Oxford in good faith and for information only. Oxford disclaims any responsibility for the materials contained in any third party website referenced in this work.

Running

Read the text below and answer the questions that follow.

"I hate Sports Day," James said to his friend Sam.

"I don't get why. You're the best runner ever and you're guaranteed to win. Who can beat you? Why are you worried?" Sam replied.

"It's not that," James said before adding, "It's just not fair. I keep telling Mum that I'm running and I want her to see me. She says she always has   5 to work, but everyone else has their family turn up." He nodded towards the seated area. Sam turned to look as the empty seats began filling up. Like a stream of ants, parents and grandparents appeared before each school year filed out. The youngest children were over-excited at their first Sports Day and the older year groups chatted and yawned, glad for the   10 sunshine and the opportunity to miss lessons.

"One day she might turn up. She could be coming today – you never know," Sam said.

"Yeah, right!" James replied.

"Hey, are you going to football tonight?" Sam asked James.   15

"Yeah, I've got my football kit with me so I can play. Are you going?"

"Of course," Sam replied, but before he could say anything more Mr Nash, the head of PE, jogged across the field to the huddle of boys.

"Right, are we all ready?" Mr Nash asked.

The boys sat in rows around the field waiting for their competition to be   20 announced. James felt nervous as he wiped his clammy hands over his shorts. It felt as if a cloud of butterflies was fluttering in his tummy and he hoped that his race would be called soon. He loved running more than anything, but he hated being watched by strangers.

"Year 5 for the four-hundred metres," shouted Mr Nash.   25

Although he felt nervous, James jumped up. He stood just behind the white line and looked at the other boys he was competing against. The whistle blew and like a bullet, James flew as fast as his legs would carry

him. He pumped his arms up and down like pistons, willing his body to
perform and then, all of a sudden, his mind and body came together
in one wonderful state. James forgot about his mum not being there, 30
he forgot about his nerves, he forgot about anyone watching him. He
forgot about football, he forgot about everything and his mind felt rested
and soothed. He felt the cool breeze against his hot forehead, he felt
weightless, effortless and he ran not for anyone else, not even for himself, 35
but because his body wanted nothing more than to run. He ran as if
this were a sprint. He crossed the finishing line, ahead of any other boy
and still he continued to run. He didn't care that hundreds of eyes were
watching him in amazement. He didn't care that Mr Nash was shouting
his name. He didn't care anymore that his mum wasn't watching him. He 40
didn't care about anything. The gentle breeze was delicious, the steady
rhythm of his body was calming and James never wanted the feeling to
stop, and so he continued to run.

Teachers looked at one another with shocked faces. Parents and pupils
could not take their eyes off James and nobody could continue with 45
Sports Day until he stopped. Mr Nash began running at the side of James
trying to talk to him, but he could not keep up with the pace; James
was a long distance runner. Then he saw her. She was on her own to the
right of the crowd. No doubt she had turned up late, but it didn't matter;
Mum had turned up after all. James stopped running and the crowd of 50
parents, pupils and teachers not only clapped, they cheered, creating
a thunderous noise. James only focused on one person clapping and
cheering and that was all he needed to hear. James wiped his hot face
with the back of his hand and then crossed back to Sam, a huge grin
spread right across his face. 55

(A) Look at the description of the moments before the race begins. Why does James hate
Sports Day?

Give **two** reasons. [2]

_____

_____

_____

2

(B) What is referred to as *Like a stream of ants*? [1]

_____

_____

(C) According to the text, how does the reader know that James is nervous before the race begins? Give **two** examples. [2]

_____

_____

(D) Find and copy a group of words that shows the moment James relaxes into the race. [1]

_____

_____

(E) Look at the text box and complete the description by writing **one** word in each answer box. [1]

Sentence	Description
he pumped his arms up and down like...	
his mind felt rested and...	
he felt...	
The gentle breeze was...	

(F) *He felt the cool breeze against his hot forehead*

Think of **three** reasons why James might have a hot forehead. [2]

_____

_____

_____

(G) Explain why the teachers looked at one another with shocked faces. [1]

_____

_____

(H) *but he could not keep up with the pace*

What does this tell you about the way James was running? [1]

_____

_____

(I) How do the younger and older children feel about Sports Day?

Tick **two** correct answers. [1]

The younger children cannot wait for the races to start. ☐

The older children cannot wait for the races to start. ☐

The younger children are relaxed in the sun and are glad to be outside. ☐

The older children are relaxed in the sun and are glad to be outside. ☐

(J) Look at the last sentence. How do these words make the reader feel? [1]

_____

_____

(K) Find and copy a group of words that shows the reason why James runs. [1]

_____

_____

(L) *Mr Nash, the head of PE, jogged across the field to the **huddle** of boys.*

In this sentence, which word is closest in meaning to the word *huddle*? Circle **one.** [1]

cuddle   curdle   cluster   clasp

Hop, Skip, Jump

Read the texts below and answer the questions that follow.

Questions & Answers

Q. Why is skipping recommended for children?

A. Playground skipping is a fantastic physical activity. So many children do not fit much exercise into their lives, but skipping is a great way to keep our bodies healthy. Skipping doesn't require special clothes; it can be played alone or with as many friends as you want. It suits all abilities, shapes, sizes and ages.

Q. Doesn't skipping require a special rope?

A. No, any rope would work and can be bought for only a few pounds. In fact, many of the shops that sell items for a pound sell skipping ropes.

Q. Is it difficult to learn how to skip?

A. No! If you are skipping alone, you hold the rope handles to the sides of your body, turn the rope and jump over it as it reaches your feet. If you are skipping with friends, you jump into the space when the rope is high up and then jump over the rope as it reaches your feet. It doesn't take long to learn.

Five Facts About Skipping

1 Ropes were made from hemp, cotton or other natural materials, but many ropes are now made from nylon or polyester.

2 Ancient Egypt and China have a history of skipping many hundreds of years ago.

3 Children in England began skipping in the 1600s.

4 There is a skipping style that uses two or more ropes to jump over.

5 Many sportspeople use skipping as a beneficial warm up and to keep fit.

Unit 2

Popular Skipping Rhymes

These rhymes are often chanted when you skip and some of them are many years old so your parents and grandparents may remember them!

Group skipping rhymes

Monkeys on the bed

Two little monkeys jumping on the bed,
One fell off and bumped his head,
Mother called the doctor and the doctor said,
"No more monkeys jumping on the bed!"

This is for a group of skippers, so for each new round a new skipper jumps in to make 'Three little monkeys', and so on.

Granny's in the kitchen

Granny's in the kitchen
Doing a little knitting
In comes (name of skipper)
And pushes her out.

This is for a group of skippers, so each skipper takes it in turn to become 'Granny' and gets pushed out by the new skipper.

Skipping rhymes for one skipper

Jump! Jump!

Jump on tippy toes, Jump! Jump!
Open leg star jumps, Jump! Jump!
Right leg only, Jump! Jump!
Left leg only, Jump! Jump!
Turn around, Jump! Jump!
Touch the ground, Jump! Jump!
Cross the rope, Jump! Jump!
Start again, Jump! Jump!

The rhyme tells you which actions the skipper performs.

Teddy Bear, Teddy Bear

Teddy bear, teddy bear, turn around
Teddy bear, teddy bear, touch the ground
Teddy bear, teddy bear, touch your nose
Teddy bear, teddy bear, touch your toes
Teddy bear, teddy bear, turn off the light
Teddy bear, teddy bear, say goodnight.

The rhyme tells you which actions the skipper performs.

9

Ⓐ Tick the following statements to show whether they are **true** or **false**. [1]

	True	False
Skipping can be played alone or with friends.		
Skipping ropes can cost under £2.		
It is quite difficult to learn how to skip.		

Ⓑ Find and copy a group of **eight** words from the text that tells us how skipping is suitable for all children. [1]

_____

_____

Ⓒ Reread the 'Questions & Answers' text. Tick the following statements to show whether they are **fact** or **opinion**. [1]

	Fact	Opinion
Skipping is great fun.		
Many people can skip at the same time.		
Skipping is the best form of exercise.		

Ⓓ Find **three** examples from the text that show us that skipping is a healthy activity. [3]

_____

_____

Ⓔ Read 'Five Facts About Skipping'. Find **four** materials that rope can be made from. [1]

_____

_____

Ⓕ Read the section 'Five Facts About Skipping'.

Find **three** countries that are mentioned in the text. [1]

_____

_____

8

(G) *Many sportspeople use skipping as a **beneficial** warm up*

Circle the word below which is closest in meaning to the word *beneficial* in this sentence. [1]

bad   good   cheap   expensive

(H) Look at the section 'Popular Skipping Rhymes'. Which **two** rhymes have actions for the skipper to do? [1]

_____

(I) Find **two** examples in the text that tell us how old the popular skipping rhymes are. [2]

_____

_____

(J) *These rhymes are often **chanted** when you skip.*

Circle the word below which is closest in meaning to the word *chanted* in this sentence. [1]

played   prayed   wrung   sung

(K) Look again at the rhyme 'Jump! Jump!'

Draw a line to match each part of the rhyme with the action needed. [1]

Touch the ground, Jump! Jump!	Hopping on the right leg
Open leg star jumps, Jump! Jump!	Placing the right hand over the left hand
Cross the rope, Jump! Jump!	Jumping with feet apart
Right leg only, Jump! Jump!	Placing fingers on the floor

(L) Look again at the 'Granny's in the kitchen' rhyme.

Which group of words tell us when *'Granny'* has to leave the skipping rope? [1]

_____

7

Sloths

Read the text below and answer the questions that follow.

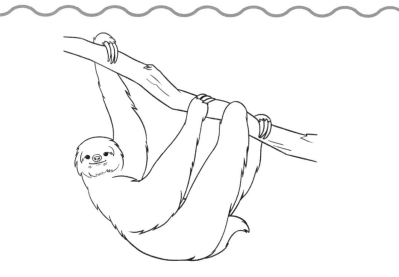

The Sloth

Bradypus tridactylus
Which is Greek for slow feet.
I am the slowest mammal;
But don't I look so sweet?

My mouth is always smiling   5
My eyes are always kind.
My long, thin claws are like fingers
As around the branch they wind.

Algae grows upon my fur
So I am grey with a hint of green,   10
I think it looks so fashionable,
And it stops me from being seen.

In Central and South America
Is where sloths can be found.
But you will never see us,   15
By walking on the ground.

Walking is too hard for us,
So I live up in my tree,
My enemies will walk on by,
If they cannot see me!   20

I spend my time eating leaves
But they're so tough to chew,
My stomach's divided into four,
So the leaves can process through.

I sleep hanging from a branch   25
Or curled up into a ball.
I know it sounds quite scary,
But I never, ever fall.

I have so little energy
I sleep for much of the day,   30
But I am an excellent swimmer
I love to splash and play!

Baby sloths stay with their mum,
Until they're four years old.
I like to cuddle up to mine,   35
She stops me feeling cold.

But one day when I'm older,
I shall find my own tree.
Then I will have a baby sloth
To cuddle up to me.   40

(A) What does *Bradypus tridactylus* mean? [1]

_____

(B) What kind of animal is a sloth?
Tick **one.** [1]

reptile ☐

bird ☐

mammal ☐

fish ☐

2

(c) Give **three** reasons why a sloth might look sweet. [3]

_____

_____

_____

(D) Why is the sloth's stomach divided into four? [1]

_____

_____

_____

(E) *So I am grey with a **hint** of green.*

Tick the word below which is closest in meaning to the word *hint* in this sentence. Tick **one**. [1]

touch	☐
sound	☐
smell	☐
feel	☐

(F) Tick the following statements to show whether they are **true** or **false**. [1]

	True	False
The sloth is happy in the water.		
Sloths only live for 4 years.		
The sloth lives at the foot of the tree.		
The sloth's food is hard to eat.		

6

(G) How does the sloth protect itself? Find **two** examples. [2]

_____

_____

(H) *I like to **cuddle** up to mine.*

Tick the word below which is closest in meaning to the word *cuddle* in this sentence. Tick **one**. [1]

face ☐

chat ☐

hog ☐

hug ☐

(I) Circle the word below that is used in the poem to mean 'foes'.
Circle **one**. [1]

cold   enemies   fashionable   process

(J) Give **two** ways in which the sloth sleeps. [2]

_____

_____

(K) Why will the sloth find another tree in the future? [1]

_____

_____

_____

7

Pond Dipping

Read the text below and answer the questions that follow.

Pond Dipping For Beginners!

This week in *Young Naturalist Magazine* we show you how to go pond dipping safely and effectively. Many people interested in life sciences will have pond dipped, but it is far more than just waving a stick or a net in the water. We show you how…

Items to Take:

1 Pond dipping net
2 A pair of old tights
3 A waterproof observation tray or large plastic box
4 A pencil and notepad
5 A ruler or tape measure

Placing one leg of a pair of old tights inside your fishing net means that little creatures can't get trapped in the mesh of the net. A camera is really useful to capture your pond life, but drawing pictures and taking measurements also help you to identify the pond life that you find.

How to Pond Dip Safely

- First of all, always make sure that the pond is a safe place to explore.   5

- NEVER go too close to the water's edge and be careful if the ground is muddy; it can be slippery.

- ALWAYS pond dip with an adult who can help you to remain safe.

- Some people prefer to sit or kneel down with   10
  their net and other people stand up. NEVER over-stretch as you can easily fall in.

- Move away from the water's edge to observe your pond life so that you don't fall in.

- Cover any cuts with a waterproof plaster to   15
  protect against infection.

- Wash your hands well with soap and water when you have finished pond dipping.

How to Pond Dip Effectively

Before you dip your net, watch the pond first. You might see all manner of wildlife when the pond is quiet and still. Fill your observation tray with pond water so that it is ready to support pond life.   20
Now you are ready to slowly dip your net into the water. Move the net very slowly three or four times in a long oval or figure of eight before gently lifting it up and placing the net in your observation tray. Now you can either take photographs, or draw pictures of your pond life for looking up later.

Don't forget to replace all of the pond life back into the water. You should always aim to cause no damage or stress to the little creatures that you find. However tempting, it is wrong to take   25
anything home with you other than your drawings and observations. In fact, some people like to draw the plant life and visiting wildlife rather than dipping a net into the water!

Turn over now to read our interview with a specialist…

(A) What is the name of the magazine? [1]

_____

(B) What stops pond life from getting stuck in the net? [1]

_____

(C) Find and copy **three** ways that you can use to identify pond life. [3]

_____

_____

_____

(D) Draw lines to match the safety advice to the risks below. [1]

If the ground is muddy	You might catch an infection
If you don't cover open cuts	You might get into danger
If you over-stretch	You might slip
If you don't have an adult near	You might fall into the water

(E) Why should you watch the pond before putting in your net?
Tick **one**. [1]

It can stop you from falling in. ☐

It can help you get your balance. ☐

You might see more wildlife. ☐

Pond life creatures hate noise. ☐

7

(F) Give **two** reasons why pond life should go back into the water. [2]

_____

_____

(G) Tick the following statements to show whether they are **true** or **false**. [1]

	True	False
Pond life can be taken home if you look after it.		
You can kneel down to dip your net in a pond.		
You should always keep your net still when it is in the pond.		
The article appears on a website.		

(H) Find and copy **one** sentence that tells you what the text aims to do. [1]

_____

_____

(I) _A waterproof **observation** tray or large plastic box_

Tick the word below which is closest in meaning to the word _observation_ in this sentence.

Tick **one**. [1]

stationed ☐

serving ☐

lightweight ☐

viewing ☐

(J) Why do you think that the text tells you to _wash your hands well with soap and water when you have finished pond dipping_? [1]

_____

_____

6

(K) Why should you fill the observation tray with pond water?
Tick **one**. [1]

To make it easier for you to see the pond life ☐

To make it more comfortable for the pond life ☐

To make it safer for you to use your net ☐

To make the observation tray more stable ☐

(L) Look at the section 'Items to Take'. Tick **one** word which is used to mean *recognise* in the text. [1]

capture ☐

identify ☐

taking ☐

measure ☐

(M) The magazine gives two different ways in which pond-dippers could move their nets. Can you draw one of the shapes that they would form here? [1]

3

The Garden

Read the text below and answer the questions that follow.

Lily had had a bad day. She didn't have any friends at that time as the other children in school were always making friends then breaking friends and it made her feel sad. On top of that, today Lily had missed her afternoon playtime because she had been talking when Mrs Suffield had asked for the class to be quiet. Mrs Suffield had said she was "very 5 disappointed" in her behaviour. To top it all, Lily scraped her knee on the wall and it was stinging. She had come into the house in a bad mood and now Mum was annoyed with her. Lily changed out of her school uniform and charged into the garden. She breathed deeply as she ran down the path, through the gate and to her favourite tree. 10

Dad had thrown a rope over the branches of an old, gnarled tree and Lily loved clambering up the rope to sit on the lowest branch. There were a number of fairy doors attached to the thick tree trunk. There was a special fairy door where Lily sat and this was where all of her secrets, worries and problems were whispered. She liked telling the fairies her concerns and she 15 was always relieved when the problems were resolved.

Today, Lily scrambled up the rope and settled herself down. From here she could see for so many kilometres and in the distance, between the trees and buildings, she could see endless fields. She could also peer into the next-door neighbours' gardens. On one side she could watch Roy, 20 who was picking long, green, curly beans for his supper. Lily kept hoping that he would turn around and see her. Roy always waved, but he was concentrating on the beans today and filling the basket that was plonked on the bench. On the other side, Lily could see Rosie's chickens foraging around, pecking bits of food wherever they could find it. Lily loved the 25 chickens. When she was younger, she used to search around Rosie's garden hunting for eggs. Rosie wouldn't get home for ages; she always went to the gym straight from work on a Wednesday.

Today, Lily had a lot of things to tell the fairies. If she couldn't talk to Roy or Rosie, she would tell the fairies instead. Lily twirled a leaf between her 30 fingers and began talking. She chatted about her friends, Mrs Suffield, grazing her knee, upsetting Mum. She couldn't stop talking. When she had finally finished telling the fairies, she followed her usual routine of tracing her finger around the little red fairy door and then gently tapping it three times.

35

Mum looked out of the window at a happy little girl who was cartwheeling and doing handstands across the lawn. Mum shook her head and tried to understand how Lily could turn from such a cross, grumpy girl to a little ray of smiling sunshine, but she was just pleased that her daughter was back to her usual happy self. Lily saw Mum smiling at the kitchen window and her heart felt light. The fairies always sorted out the problem. Lily was amazed as she tried to understand how they could have turned Mum from such a cross, grumpy adult to a lovely smiling one, but she was just pleased that Mum was back to her usual happy self. She skipped into the kitchen and hugged Mum.

40

If you had been standing under the tree at the bottom of the garden that day, and had listened very carefully, you would have heard a gentle noise on the breeze that sounded a lot like laughter...

45

Ⓐ Read the first paragraph. Why was Lily feeling sad?

Give **one** reason. [1]

_____

_____

_____

Ⓑ Why couldn't Lily speak to Roy?
Tick **one**. [1]

Lily could not see him.	☐
Roy was busy collecting food from the garden.	☐
Roy went to the gym on a Wednesday.	☐
Lily had missed her afternoon play time.	☐

2

(c) According to the text, how does the reader know that Lily is sometimes worried? [1]

_____ 6

_____

(d) Find and copy a group of **nine** words that shows the reader that Lily is not normally sad. [1]

_____

_____

(e) Tick the following statements to show whether they are **true** or **false**. [1]

	True	False
A bee had stung Lily's knee.		
Mr Suffield was Lily's teacher.		
She tapped a red fairy door four times.		
Lily's garden had a lawn, a path and a gate.		

(f) *she was always relieved when the problems were **resolved***

Tick the word or phrase below which is closest in meaning to the word *resolved* in this sentence.

Tick **one**. [1]

put right   ☐

made smaller   ☐

ignored   ☐

made worse   ☐

(g) Find and copy **two** words that are used in the text to mean 'climb'. [2]

_____

_____

6

(H) How did Lily change from the beginning of the text to the end? [2]

_____ 6

_____

_____

_____

(I) Which words best describe the tree? Tick **two**. [1]

The tree had been growing for a long time. ☐

The tree had been planted by Dad. ☐

The tree was tall and slender. ☐

The tree was twisted and stout. ☐

(J) *Lily could see Rosie's chickens **foraging** around, pecking bits of food wherever they could find it.*

Circle the word below which is closest in meaning to the word *foraging* in this sentence. Circle **one**. [1]

flying   hunting   squawking   eating

(K) What do you think the sound is at the end of the text? Tick **one**. [1]

Lily laughing as she did cartwheels and handstands ☐

Mum laughing as she watches Lily ☐

The fairies laughing as Lily and Mum were now happy ☐

The wind blowing ☐

(L) What **two** things did Lily always do when she had finished talking to the fairies? [1]

_____

_____

_____

Answers

Unit 1

(A) 1 mark for each: James hated being watched by strangers / James didn't have his mum there to watch him. [2]

(B) The *parents and grandparents* spectating were *like a stream of ants*. [1]

(C) 1 mark for any two: *James felt nervous / James wiped his clammy hands over his shorts / James felt as if a cloud of butterflies was fluttering in his tummy / Although he felt nervous* [2]

(D) *his mind and body came together in one wonderful state.* [1]

(E) All correct for 1 mark: *he pumped his arms up and down like* pistons / *his mind felt rested and* soothed / *he felt* weightless / *The gentle breeze was* delicious. [1]

(F) 1 mark for any two; 2 marks for all three: The weather was hot / James was nervous / James was hot from running. [2]

(G) 1 mark for any one: The teachers looked shocked because they were amazed at James' fantastic running ability / The race was over but James still kept running. [1]

(H) James was running so fast that even the PE teacher could not keep up with him. [1]

(I) All correct for 1 mark: The younger children cannot wait for the races to start / The older children are relaxed in the sun and are glad to be outside. [1]

(J) The reader feels happy that James has what he always wanted, as his mum could watch him. [1]

(K) 1 mark for any one: *his mind and body came together in one wonderful state / because his body wanted nothing more than to run / he loved running more than anything* [1]

(L) cluster [1]

Unit 2

(A) All correct for 1 mark: True, True, False [1]

(B) *It suits all abilities, shapes, sizes and ages* [1]

(C) All correct for 1 mark: Opinion, Fact, Opinion [1]

(D) 1 mark for each: *Playground skipping is a fantastic physical activity / Skipping is a great way to keep our bodies healthy / Many sportspeople use skipping as a beneficial warm up and to keep fit* [3]

(E) All correct for 1 mark: *hemp, cotton, nylon, polyester* [1]

(F) All correct for 1 mark: *(Ancient) Egypt, China, England* [1]

(G) good [1]

(H) All correct for 1 mark: 'Jump! Jump!' and 'Teddy Bear, Teddy Bear' [1]

(I) 1 mark for each: *some of them are many years old / your parents and grandparents may remember them* [2]

(J) sung [1]

(K) All correctly matched for 1 mark: Touch the ground, Jump! Jump! = Placing fingers on the floor / Open leg star jumps, Jump! Jump! = Jumping with feet apart / Cross the rope, Jump! Jump! = Placing the right hand over the left hand / Right leg only, Jump! Jump! = Hopping on the right leg [1]

(L) *In comes (name of skipper) And pushes her out.* [1]

Unit 3

(A) *Bradypus tridactylus* means slow feet in Greek. [1]

(B) mammal [1]

(C) 1 mark for each: The sloth's mouth *is always smiling /* The sloth's eyes *are always kind /* The sloth likes to *cuddle up* to its mother. [3]

(D) So that the tough leaves which it eats can be processed. [1]

(E) touch [1]

(F) All correct for 1 mark: True, False, False, True [1]

(G) 1 mark for each: The sloth is protected by the algae growing on the fur which *stops [it] from being seen /* By living up in the tree the *enemies walk on by*. [2]

(H) hug [1]

(I) enemies [1]

(J) 1 mark for each: The sloth sleeps hanging from a branch / The sloth curls up into a ball. [2]

(K) The sloth will be old enough to leave her mum and can then have her own baby. [1]

Unit 4

(A) *Young Naturalist Magazine* [1]

(B) Putting one leg of a pair of old tights inside the net. [1]

(C) 1 mark for each: Use *a camera / drawing pictures / taking measurements*. [3]

(D) All correctly matched for 1 mark: If the ground is muddy = you might slip / If you don't cover open cuts = you might catch an infection / If you over-stretch = you might fall into the water / If you don't have an adult near = you might get into danger. [1]

(E) You might see more wildlife. [1]

(F) 1 mark for each: You are *aiming to cause no damage or stress to the little creatures that you find* / *It is wrong to take anything home with you*. [2]

(G) All correct for 1 mark: False, True, False, False [1]

(H) *This week in* Young Naturalist Magazine *we show you how to go pond dipping safely and effectively.* [1]

(I) viewing [1]

(J) Pond water is dirty so you need to wash them with soap and water to remove any dirt and germs to stop infection. [1]

(K) To make it more comfortable for the pond life. [1]

(L) identify [1]

(M) Child's own drawing of a figure of eight or an oval, e.g.:
⬭ ∞ [1]

Unit 5

(A) 1 mark for any one: Lily *didn't really have any friends* / *Lily had missed her afternoon play time* / *Mrs Suffield was very disappointed* in her / *Lily's knee was hurting* / *Mum was annoyed* with Lily. [1]

(B) Roy was busy collecting food from the garden. [1]

(C) 1 mark for any one: The text states, *where all of her secrets, worries and problems were whispered* or *Lily liked telling the fairies her concerns.* [1]

(D) *Her daughter was back to her usual happy self.* [1]

(E) All correct for 1 mark: False, False, False, True. [1]

(F) put right [1]

(G) All correct for 1 mark: clambering / scrambled [2]

(H) 1 mark for recognising that Lily was sad and in a bad mood at the beginning of the text and 1 mark for recognising that Lily was happy at the end of the text. [2]

(I) Both correct for 1 mark: The tree had been growing for a long time / The tree was twisted and stout. [1]

(J) hunting [1]

(K) The fairies laughing as Lily and Mum were now happy. (Lily and Mum were in the kitchen and the sound is *on the breeze* so it cannot be the wind.) [1]

(L) All correct for 1 mark: Lily always traced her finger around the little red fairy door and then she gently tapped the door three times. [1]

Unit 6

(A) People remained in one place instead of living a nomadic life so it became worth investing time and money in growing crops and keeping animals in one location. [1]

(B) It makes the soil lighter (it breaks up heavy soil). [1]

(C) 1 mark for each: A device to sow seed in straight lines / A hoe to get rid of weeds between the rows of plants. [2]

(D) 1 mark for each: Animals couldn't be kept over the winter as there was not enough food for them / Growing swedes and turnips to feed the animals meant they could live through the winter time / Because of this, animals could grow larger so they more useful to farmers and more profitable. [3]

(E) lacking [1]

(F) All correct for 1 mark: True, False, True, True [1]

(G) Brought into the UK from other countries. [1]

(H) 1 mark for each: Railways helped people move to the towns, so markets were needed to feed the people living in the towns / The railways helped move goods around so farm produce could be taken from the countryside into towns. [2]

(I) Both correct for 1 mark: Machines were more efficient than workers and animals / Pesticides and fertilisers were used by farmers. [1]

(J) All correctly matched for 1 mark: A farm with Christmas trees = Growing different products / A farm with llamas = Keeping different animals / A farm with mazes for people to complete = Encouraging visitors / A farm with a bakery = Using and selling produce. [1]

(K) 1 mark for any one: In the first sentence Old MacDonald had the traditional farm animals but in the final sentence, Old MacDonald has the traditional farm animals but she also has a range of other sources of income such as selling or using honey, fruit and providing accommodation for holidaymakers / We may also assume at the beginning that Old MacDonald is male, but at the end of the passage is referred to as 'she'. [1]

Unit 7

(A) Boo Boo is a bear (she has claws and paws, visits teddy bear shops and loves honey). [1]

(B) All in the correct order for 1 mark: 1: The invitation arrives / 2: Boo Boo goes shopping / 3: Boo Boo and Winnie have a sleepover / 4: Boo Boo tastes honey covered apples. [1]

(C) All correct for 2 marks: flip-flops / anoraks / shirts / suits. [2]

(D) stylish [1]

(E) 1 mark for the first answer and 1 mark for any two of the following: No they did not go to bed early / On Saturday Boo Boo was so tired / They chatted until they were too tired to talk / They watched the films, then painted their claws and then chatted. [2]

(F) The onesie made her look like a penguin. [1]

(G) Boo Boo and Winnie painted their claws so that their paws matched. [1]

(H) 1 mark each for any two: *How very exciting / I LOVE picnics! / I CANNOT WAIT / The picnic was fantastic* [2]

(I) 1 mark for each. [3]

When was the picnic?	The picnic was on Sunday
What did Boo Boo hope to see at the picnic?	Boo Boo hoped to see her favourite food at the picnic
What decision does Boo Boo have to make?	Boo Boo had to decide what to wear

(J) Thursday was tiring as Boo Boo went shopping and tried on so many clothes. [1]

Unit 8

(A) 1 mark each for any four: *It looks beautiful when it is laden with blossom* / It guarantees *a heavy crop of plums* / The wood *can be used to make beautifully carved items* / The wood can make *firewood* / The plum fruit *can be eaten fresh off the tree* / The plum fruit can be *used in so many recipes* / The plums are healthy. [4]

(B) Leaving the wood to dry before using it. [1]

(C) All correct for 1 mark: True, True, False, True [1]

(D) They have lots of vitamins and nutrients in them. (The other reasons are all true of plums but they are not directly related to our diet and usefulness in our diet.) [1]

(E) loaded [1]

(F) All correct for 1 mark: Opinion, Opinion, Fact, Fact [1]

(G) *There is evidence that they are one of the first fruits that early humans ate.* [1]

(H) A glass bowl allows you to see the different layers of fruit, yoghurt and muesli. [1]

(I) change [1]

(J) 1 mark for any one: You can use any fruit that you want / You can use any yoghurt that you want / You can use porridge oats or crushed ginger biscuits / You can eat the dessert immediately or after chilling it in the fridge / The dessert can be eaten as a dessert or for breakfast. [1]

(K) Fantastic Fruity Layers is the best title as the dessert does not have custard, it isn't a cake, it isn't frozen but it is built in layers. [1]

(L) Answer could be 'Yes' or 'No', with one suitable reason given such as: 'Yes' because a plum is a fruit / A plum has lots of nutrients / A plum has more vitamin A than 9 portions of apples / A plum has more vitamin C than 2 portions of carrots / A plum has more fibre than 3 portions of mango / A plum has fewer calories than $\frac{1}{2}$ a portion of banana / A plum has no fat in it. 'No' because a plum still has sugar in it and too much sugar is bad for our health / There might be other fruit or vegetables with better nutrients / There might be other fruit or vegetables with fewer calories. [1]

Unit 9

(A) He was hungry but everyone seemed to be taking ages. [1]

(B) Caleb swiped at the barbecue with his stick which caused it to topple to the ground. [1]

(C) 1 mark each for any two: He felt dizzy / He was not in his own bed / His head felt sore / His grandparents and dad were watching over him. [2]

(D) All in the correct order for 1 mark: 1: The family were looking at Jethro's school report / 2: Caleb found a lightsabre / 3: Grandma was crying / 4: Caleb had his stitches removed. [1]

(E) wiped [1]

(F) All correct for 1 mark: True, False, True, False [1]

(G) *Your head is all bandaged up as you had to have some stitches for a deep cut on your head.* [1]

(H) 1 mark each for any two: Caleb's parents could sleep over next to Caleb / Caleb was going to be okay / Caleb's grandparents would look after everything at home. [2]

(I) There will be a trip to the theatre / There will be food available. [1]

(J) dawdling [1]

Unit 10

(A) 1 mark each for any three observations from the following: *The ivy lies thick / Swirls and twirls of leaves and twine Wind around each other like a knitted knot* [3]

(B) The sound of the baby blackbirds. [1]

(C) 1 mark for each: *fluffy / plump* [2]

(D) smallest [1]

(E) All correct for 1 mark: True, False, False, True [1]

(F) *light greenish blue with rich brown spots* [1]

(G) A predator is a creature that hunts and kills another. [1]

(H) All correctly matched for 1 mark: Blackbirds singing at the end of the day = will carry messages to the dead / Blackbirds nesting near a house = will bring a year of good luck / A blackbird singing when looking at you = will teach you an important lesson / Two male blackbirds sitting together = will bring good luck. [1]

(I) *colly bird* [1]

(J) 1 mark each for any two: A blackbird brings good luck / A blackbird teaches us a lesson / A blackbird passes messages to people who are dead. [2]

(K) *Blackbirds feature in many different myths, legends, stories and superstitions.* [1]

Old MacDonald Had a Farm

Read the text below and answer the questions that follow.

We know that Old MacDonald had cows, sheep, horses, pigs, goats, ducks and hens, but how much do we really know about farms?

People began farming over 11 000 years ago when, instead of gathering and hunting food, they began to grow crops and raise animals. They could now do this because they remained in one place instead of living a   5
nomadic life, frequently moving and taking all their possessions with them.

Although there was the invention of the plough – a tool to help break up heavy soil – and the discovery of new crops such as potatoes, farming did not really change much until the 1700s. In 1701 a man called Jethro Tull invented a device to sow seed in straight lines and a hoe to get rid of the   10
weeds between rows of plants.

There were other changes in farming. Farmers began to grow turnips and swedes that they could use as animal feed. Charles 'Turnip' Townshend used this technique which made a huge difference. Until then, animals could not be kept over the winter and early spring because there was   15
not enough food to keep the animals alive. Now that farm animals could be kept for longer, they could grow larger and become more useful and profitable.

Farming continued to change with the Industrial Revolution because as towns grew and railways helped people and goods to move around,   20
so markets were needed where farmers could sell as much produce as they could grow. Lots of machines were invented to make farming easier, but there were also difficulties in farming. Railways and ships meant that other countries could ship their produce to Britain and as soon as refrigeration was possible, meat could be imported from abroad.   25

Foreign imports could have made farming impossible, as could the two world wars that encouraged Britain to 'Dig for Victory' and to turn every garden and patch of bare land into a profitable plot for growing fruit and vegetables. Instead, pesticides and artificial fertilizers helped farmers to make the most of intensive farming and as tractors and combine 30 harvesters replaced horses and oxen, fewer people were needed to do the same job. That is not to say that farming was easy. It has always been an extremely difficult job.

What is farming like today? Well, there is a development in genetically engineered crops to produce food for countries that have problems 35 with insufficient food. In Britain, there is a return to organic farming and farmers having to have more than one source of income to survive. Some farmers encourage visitors by providing bed and breakfast, having campsites on their land, holding music or arts festivals, making mazes in fields of crops or creating quad bike courses. Some dairy farmers use their 40 produce to make products such as ice-cream or even soap and toiletries, while sheep farmers might sell knitted clothing and arable farmers might sell bread and cakes or beer made from their grain. Some farmers have succeeded by simply growing different products from the traditional, such as biofuel crops, flowers, Christmas trees or keeping animals such as 45 llamas, alpacas or giant rabbits.

Old MacDonald might still have cows, sheep, horses, pigs, goats, ducks and hens, but she might also have beehives, an orchard and a field full of holidaymakers.

Ⓐ Why did people begin to grow crops and to keep animals? [1]

_____

_____

Ⓑ What is the best description of what a plough does?
Tick **one.** [1]

It makes the soil richer. ☐

It makes the soil wetter. ☐

It makes the soil lighter. ☐

It makes the soil heavier. ☐

ⓒ What **two** things did Jethro Tull create? [2]

_____

_____

ⓓ Give **three** reasons why Charles 'Turnip' Townshend's technique made a huge difference to farming. [3]

_____

_____

_____

_____

ⓔ *for countries that have problems with **insufficient** food*

Circle the word below which is closest in meaning to the word *insufficient* in this sentence. Circle **one**. [1]

satisfactory   surplus   lacking   healthy

ⓕ Tick the following statements to show whether they are **true** or **false**. [1]

	True	False
Some farms today grow crops that can be used for fuel.		
The Industrial Revolution had no impact on farming.		
People were farming in the year 1150.		
People grew fruit and vegetables wherever possible during wartime.		

ⓖ *meat could be **imported** from abroad*

Tick the phrase below which is closest in meaning to the word *imported* in this sentence. Tick **one**. [1]

Sent from the UK to other countries   ☐

Brought into the UK from other countries   ☐

Remained in port   ☐

Kept away from port   ☐

8

Ⓗ How did the railways change farming? Find **two** examples. [2]

_____

_____

_____

_____

Ⓘ Why did farming remain possible during wartime? Tick **two** reasons. [1]

Machines were more efficient than workers and animals. ☐

Every homeowner grew their own produce. ☐

Pesticides and fertilisers were used by farmers. ☐

'Dig for Victory' asked people to support farmers. ☐

Ⓙ Draw lines to match each farm with the ways in which it could create further income. [1]

A farm with Christmas trees	Encouraging visitors
A farm with llamas	Using and selling produce
A farm with mazes for people to complete	Growing different products
A farm with a bakery	Keeping different animals

Ⓚ How has the Old MacDonald in the last sentence changed from the Old MacDonald in the opening sentence? [1]

_____

_____

_____

5

The Teddy Bears' Picnic

Read the text below and answer the questions that follow.

Wednesday

An invitation arrived through the door today. How very exciting it was too! It said, "Miss Boo Boo is cordially invited to a picnic on Sunday." I LOVE picnics! I hope that my favourite food will be there. I love honey sandwiches, honey tea and yummy, yummy honey cake. I will have to decide what to wear...   5

Thursday

Well I have had such a tiring day today. I went to the teddy bear shops with my dear friend Rupert to find something suitable to wear. I have tried on skirts and shirts, suits and boots, tops and flip-flops, anoraks and macs, frocks and socks. In the end I bought an A-M-A-Z-I-N-G onesie that makes me look like a penguin – it   10 really is hilarious! Rupert is wearing a tartan kilt with a matching scarf. He looks so elegant.

Friday

I heard from my cousin Winnie today. She is going to the picnic so that will be lovely. She is coming for a sleepover tonight. I cannot wait to show her my onesie! She is bringing her favourite film 'Yogi   15 Bear' and I have chosen 'Brother Bear' to watch tonight and then we're going to bed early.

Saturday

Oh my goodness I am so tired! Winnie and I watched our favourite films. We ate honey and beeswax pizza and honey-coated popcorn. Then we painted our claws so that we have matching paws 20 (we look super cute). Then we chatted until we were too tired to talk. We always say that we're going to sleep early but we always talk too much. Anyway, the picnic is tomorrow and I CANNOT WAIT. Now I am going to sleep zzzzzzzz.

Sunday

The picnic was fantastic. Winnie sat next to Paddington and I sat 25 between Winnie and Rupert. Everyone thought my onesie was brilliant — they all laughed! All of my favourite food was there and who knew that honey-covered apples taste soooo good? They are my new favourite food — yum!

(A) What kind of animal do you think Boo Boo is? [1]

___

(B) Number the sentences below from 1 to 4 to show the order in which they happen in the story.

The first one has been done for you. [1]

Boo Boo and Winnie have a sleepover. _____

Boo Boo goes shopping. _____

The invitation arrives. _1___

Boo Boo tastes honey-covered apples. _____

2

(c) Find the rhyming words from the text that match the words below. [2]

tops and _____

macs and _____

skirts and _____

boots and _____

(d) *He looks so **elegant***

Tick the word below which is closest in meaning to the word *elegant* in this sentence.
Tick **one**. [1]

oval ☐

tall ☐

stylish ☐

crazy ☐

(e) On Friday Boo Boo states that they are going to bed early.

Did they go to bed early? Find **two** reasons to support your answer. [2]

_____

_____

_____

_____

(f) Why did Boo Boo think that her onesie was hilarious?
Tick **one**. [1]

The onesie was too big for her. ☐

The onesie made her look like a penguin. ☐

The onesie makes her look elegant. ☐

The onesie is so amazing. ☐

6

(G) What did Boo Boo and Winnie do to make themselves look *super cute*? [1]

_____

_____

(H) Find **two** phrases which tell you how Boo Boo feels about picnics. [2]

_____

_____

(I) Look at the diary entry for Wednesday.

Complete the table about Boo Boo's invitation to the picnic. [3]

When was the picnic?	
What did Boo Boo hope to see at the picnic?	
What decision does Boo Boo have to make?	

(J) Why do you think that Thursday was such a tiring day? [1]

_____

_____

_____

7

Plums

Read the text below and answer the questions that follow.

The plum tree is an amazing little tree. It looks beautiful when it is laden with blossom. Bees buzz around the pretty flowers, pollinating the tree and guaranteeing a heavy crop of plums. The wood of the plum tree can be used to make beautifully carved items. Even the leftovers make wonderful firewood as long as it is well-seasoned, which means it needs to be left to   5
reduce the amount of moisture in it before burning.

All plums have a stone in the middle, similar to cherries and peaches. Plums can be eaten fresh off the tree but they can also be used in so many recipes from jam, chutney and drinks to pies, crumbles and cakes. Plum skins can be green, yellow, red or, most commonly, purple. There is   10
evidence that they are one of the first fruits that early humans ate.

We have heard so much about eating too much sugar, but eating fruit as part of a balanced diet is a vital way of getting all of the goodness we need each day. Here are all of the **facts** and figures according to the Netherlands Nutrition Centre to help you see how good plums are: 15

100 g of plum fruit provides:			
Calories	42 Kcal	Vitamin A	18 µg
Sugar	9.6 g	Vitamin B6	0.1 mg
Fat	0 g	Vitamin C	5 mg
Fibre	2.2 g	Vitamin E	0.7 mg

Just a 100 g portion of plums provides:
• more vitamin A than 9 portions of apple
• more vitamin C than 2 portions of carrot
• more fibre than 3 portions of mango
• fewer calories than $\frac{1}{2}$ a portion of banana   20

Here is a simple yet delicious dessert recipe. If you place it in a glass bowl you will be able to see the attractive layers. The beauty of this dessert is that you don't need to measure the ingredients and it is versatile as you can use any fruit that you want. Today, I'm using plums.

Ingredients:

1 portion per person of fresh, tinned or frozen plums cut into pieces. 25

1 portion per person of low-fat natural yoghurt – full-fat also works well.

1 portion per person of muesli – any flavour.

1. In a bowl layer $\frac{1}{3}$ of the muesli.

2. Layer $\frac{1}{4}$ of yoghurt over the muesli.

3. Layer $\frac{1}{2}$ of plums over the yoghurt. 30

4. Layer $\frac{1}{4}$ of yoghurt over the plums.

5. Layer $\frac{1}{3}$ of muesli over the yoghurt.

6. Layer $\frac{1}{4}$ of yoghurt over the muesli.

7. Layer the last of the plums over the yoghurt.

8. Layer the last of the yoghurt over the plums. 35

9. Layer the last of the muesli over the yoghurt.

The dessert can be made just before you eat it, but it is equally delicious chilled in the fridge or can be eaten for breakfast the following morning. You could vary it by using berries, banana, mango, peach or even a mix of fruit. You could change the plain yoghurt for fruit yoghurt and you 40 could swap the muesli for porridge oats or crushed ginger biscuits.

Ⓐ Why is the plum tree *an amazing little tree*?

Find **four** reasons. [4]

_____

_____

_____

_____

_____

_____

_____

4

Ⓑ What does *seasoning wood* mean? Tick **one**. [1]

Adding salt and pepper to it ☐

Using the wood immediately ☐

Leaving the wood to dry before using it ☐

Burning the wood before using it ☐

Ⓒ Tick the following statements to show whether they are **true** or **false**. [1]

	True	False
Yellow plums have a stone in them.		
You can carve the wood to make things.		
There is more than 3g of fibre in 100g of plums.		
Bananas have more than 84 calories in a portion of 100g.		

Ⓓ Why might plums be useful in our diet? Tick **one**. [1]

They are easily pollinated by bees. ☐

They are similar to cherries and peaches. ☐

They make great chutney. ☐

They have lots of vitamins and nutrients in them. ☐

Ⓔ *The plum tree looks beautiful when it is **laden** with blossom.*

Tick the word below which is closest in meaning to the word *laden* in this sentence. Tick **one**. [1]

empty ☐   painted ☐

loaded ☐   scented ☐

Ⓕ Tick the following statements to show whether they are **fact** or **opinion**. [1]

	Fact	Opinion
The plum tree looks beautiful when it is laden with blossom.		
Here is a simple yet delicious dessert recipe.		
All plums have a stone in the middle similar to cherries and peaches.		
Today, I'm using plums.		

5

G Find and copy **one** sentence that explains for how long plum trees have been used. [1]

_____

_____

H Explain why using a glass bowl is recommended in the recipe. [1]

_____

_____

I *You could **vary** it by using berries, banana, mango, peach*

Tick the word below which is closest in meaning to the word *vary* in this sentence.
Tick **one**. [1]

change ☐   tasty ☐

reduce ☐   improve ☐

J Explain why the dessert recipe is versatile. [1]

_____

_____

K Which of the following recipe titles would work best?
Tick **one**. [1]

Fabulous Fruit and Custard ☐

Fantastic Fruity Layers ☐

Fresh Fruit Cake ☐

Frozen Fruity Fluff ☐

L Do you think plums are healthy?

Give **one** reason to support your answer. [1]

_____

_____

6

Sleepover

Read the text below and answer the questions that follow.

"Keep away from the barbecue!" Caleb's dad shouted across the garden. Mum was pottering about in the kitchen making a salad and both sets of grandparents and his aunty and uncle were grabbing a drink and chatting. Even his big cousin Jethro was busy showing everyone his latest school report. Caleb was hungry, but everyone was taking ages. He sighed deeply **5** and looked at the wood burning at the bottom of the barbecue with the black coals above.

Caleb ran around the trees at the bottom of the garden and found a stick which made an amazing lightsabre. He checked if there were any bees living in his homemade bee house and then he checked if there was any **10** food yet on the barbecue. No such luck! He swiped at the barbecue with his lightsabre as he scooted past it, then darted back up the garden.

"Oh no!" shouted Dad, "The barbecue!"

Caleb turned as he ran to see the barbecue topple to the ground, sending searing hot coals and flaming wood all over the garden... and then he **15** didn't remember anything else...

***

The next time Caleb opened his eyes he felt very sleepy and dizzy. He was lying in a bed with his grandparents and Dad watching him. Grandma was crying and Dad looked tired – he had been crying too. Caleb could see that this was not his bed and his head felt very sore. **20**

"Where am I?" he asked.

Dad said, "You're at the children's hospital. You tripped and banged your head on the garden table. Your head is all bandaged up as you had to have some stitches for a deep cut on your head."

"Where's Mum?" Caleb asked, trying to turn his head to look around. **25**

"She'll be here in a sec. She was talking to the nurse about tonight."

"What's happening tonight? When can we go home?" Caleb asked.

Dad looked up as Mum came back. "What did they say?" he asked her.

"How are you feeling?" Mum asked Caleb as she leant over to kiss his cheek. "They said that you would wake up soon." She began to cry before adding, "The nurses are fantastic – and the fundraisers. People have raised enough money to make rooms where families can stay together. We just need Grandma to pop home for an overnight bag and then we can settle down for the night." 30

Caleb's face lit up. "Are we having a huge family sleepover?" 35

Dad laughed, "Son, you can have as many sleepovers as you want when we get home, but until then, it'll be you, me and your mum. Grandpa will feed the fish and Grandma will let everyone know that you're okay."

"It's a huge relief." Mum added as she dabbed her eyes with a tissue.

***

"Mum, I've got an invitation!" Caleb pushed the card in front of her. 40

"Oh wow!" Mum said, "It's from the children's hospital. There's a Christmas party and you've been invited. How lovely is that?"

Caleb had started back at school, although he still had to visit the hospital to have his stitches removed. He had been very scared about this, but in reality, it was over before he knew it. 45

"It says here," Mum continued, "there's a magician at the theatre and then a lovely meal and we're all invited. Isn't that wonderful? You can write a little note to say that we'd love to attend. Now where are your socks?"

Ⓐ Read the first paragraph. Why did Caleb sigh deeply? [1]

_____

_____

_____

_____

1

B How did the barbecue fall over? [1]

_____

_____

C When Caleb opened his eyes, how did he know that something was wrong? Find **two** reasons. [2]

_____

_____

D Number the sentences below from 1 to 4 to show the order in which they happened in the story. [1]

Caleb has his stitches removed. _____

Grandma was crying. _____

The family were looking at Jethro's school report. _____

Caleb found a lightsabre. _____

E _Mum added as she **dabbed** her eyes with a tissue_

Tick the word below which is closest in meaning to the word _dabbed_ in this sentence. Tick **one**. [1]

painted ☐

taunted ☐

wiped ☐

blew ☐

F Tick the following statements to show whether they are **true** or **false**. [1]

	True	False
Caleb made a house for bees to live in.		
Grandpa fed the dog.		
Caleb had cut his head.		
Caleb had a nephew called Jethro.		

6

(G) Find and copy **one** sentence that explains what the hospital did when Caleb was first admitted. [1]

_____

_____

_____

(H) Why did Mum say, "*It's a huge relief*"? Find **two** reasons. [2]

_____

_____

_____

_____

(I) Tick the **two** activities that will be taking place at the Christmas party. [1]

There will be a barbecue. ☐

There will be a sleepover. ☐

There will be a trip to the theatre. ☐

There will be food available. ☐

(J) *Mum was **pottering** about in the kitchen.*

Tick the word below which is closest in meaning to the word *pottering* in this sentence. Tick **one**. [1]

sculpting ☐

creating ☐

washing ☐

dawdling ☐

5

Blackbirds

Read the text below and answer the questions that follow.

Baby Blackbirds

The ivy lies thick against the garden fence.

Swirls and twirls of leaves and twine

Wind around each other like a knitted knot.

And then I spot the blackbird.

He flies onto the nearby tree branch and waits patiently.   5

Then he hops between the smallest of gaps.

I hear the tiniest of sounds.

Little "pip, pip, pip" so high and soft.

We now have four baby blackbirds.

They are greedy little things –   10

Mr Blackbird is feeding them worms from the lawn.

They eat a lot and are all fluffy and plump.

They can't yet fly, but hop around the tree.

It is the most beautiful sight to me.

Quick Guide to Blackbirds	
Feeding	Worms, insects, fruit and berries
Habitat	Woods, farmland, moorland, parks, urban areas, garden
Colour	Males are black, females are brown; beak and around the eye are yellowy-orange
Size	24–29 cm long, 35–38 cm wing span
Weight	80–125 g
Eggs	Light greenish blue with rich brown spots
Life Expectancy	2 years, but the oldest recorded age is nearly 22 years old
Predators	Cats, foxes, hawks

Blackbird Tales

Blackbirds feature in many different **myths**, **legends**, stories and **superstitions**. It is traditionally believed that seeing two male blackbirds sitting together means good luck and if blackbirds nest near to a house, that house will receive nothing but good luck all year long. Sadly though, many blackbirds learned not to nest too close to a house in case they ended up being turned into a pie, like in the nursery rhyme 'Sing a song of sixpence':

15

20

> Sing a song of sixpence, a pocket full of rye,
>
> Four and twenty blackbirds baked in a pie.
>
> When the pie was opened the birds began to sing,
>
> So wasn't that a tasty dish to set before the King?

25

Blackbirds sing beautifully in the evening time so it is said if you speak to a blackbird at this magical time, the bird will carry your message to anyone who is dead. If a blackbird is looking at you when it sings, it is believed that it is teaching you something important and valuable. Perhaps this is why blackbirds are traditionally seen as sacred and known as friends and comforters. They would have made an ideal present and in the Christmas Carol 'The Twelve Days of Christmas', the 'four calling birds' was originally written as 'four colly birds', which was a nickname for blackbirds.

30

(A) Look at the poem 'Baby Blackbirds'.

How is the ivy described? Find **three** examples to support your answer. [3]

_____

_____

_____

(B) What is the *pip, pip, pip* sound? [1]

_____

(C) Find and copy **two** words that describe what the baby blackbirds look like. [2]

_____

(D) *I hear the **tiniest** of sounds*

Tick the word below which is closest in meaning to the word *tiniest* in this sentence. Tick **one**. [1]

metallic ☐

sweetest ☐

cutest ☐

smallest ☐

(E) Look at the 'Quick Guide to Blackbirds'.

Tick the following statements to show whether they are **true** or **false**. [1]

	True	False
Blackbirds could eat strawberries, raspberries and blackberries.		
Female blackbirds are black with yellowy orange around the eye.		
A blackbird could be 135 g in weight.		
Most blackbirds don't reach their full age before they die.		

8

(F) Describe a blackbird's egg. [1]

_____

(G) What is meant by a *predator*? [1]

_____

_____

(H) Draw lines to match the blackbird behaviour below to its believed meaning. [1]

Blackbirds singing at the end of the day	Will teach you an important lesson
Blackbirds nesting near a house	Will carry messages to the dead
A blackbird singing when looking at you	Will bring good luck
Two male blackbirds sitting together	Will bring a year of good luck

(I) Look at the text 'Blackbird Tales'.

What was used as a nickname for a blackbird? [1]

_____

(J) Find **two** reasons why a blackbird might be traditionally seen as sacred, a friend and a comforter. [2]

_____

_____

_____

(K) Find and copy **one** sentence that shows us where blackbird stories can be found. [1]

_____

_____

7

Key Words

fact:
information that is true and can be proven; not someone's point of view

legend:
a story that has some truth to it, but has been exaggerated and changed over time

myth:
a story that is not true and often uses magical characters

opinion:
information that is someone's point of view and can't be proven

superstition:
a belief that some thought or action will bring good or bad luck

Progress chart

How did you do? Fill in your score below and shade in the corresponding boxes to compare your progress across the different tests and units.

	50%	100%

Unit 1, p4 Score __ / 2

Unit 1, p5 Score __ / 7

Unit 1, p6 Score __ / 6

Unit 2, p9 Score __ / 8

Unit 2, p10 Score __ / 7

Unit 3, p12 Score __ / 2

Unit 3, p13 Score __ / 6

Unit 3, p14 Score __ / 7

Unit 4, p16 Score __ / 7

Unit 4, p17 Score __ / 6

Unit 4, p18 Score __ / 3

Unit 5, p20 Score __ / 2

Unit 5, p21 Score __ / 6

Unit 5, p22 Score __ / 6

Unit 6, p28 Score __ / 2

Unit 6, p29 Score __ / 8

Unit 6, p30 Score __ / 5

Unit 7, p32 Score __ / 2

Unit 7, p33 Score __ / 6

Unit 7, p34 Score __ / 7

Unit 8, p36 Score __ / 4

Unit 8, p37 Score __ / 5

Unit 8, p38 Score __ / 6

Unit 9, p40 Score __ / 1

Unit 9, p41 Score __ / 6

Unit 9, p42 Score __ / 5

Unit 10, p45 Score __ / 8

Unit 10, p46 Score __ / 7